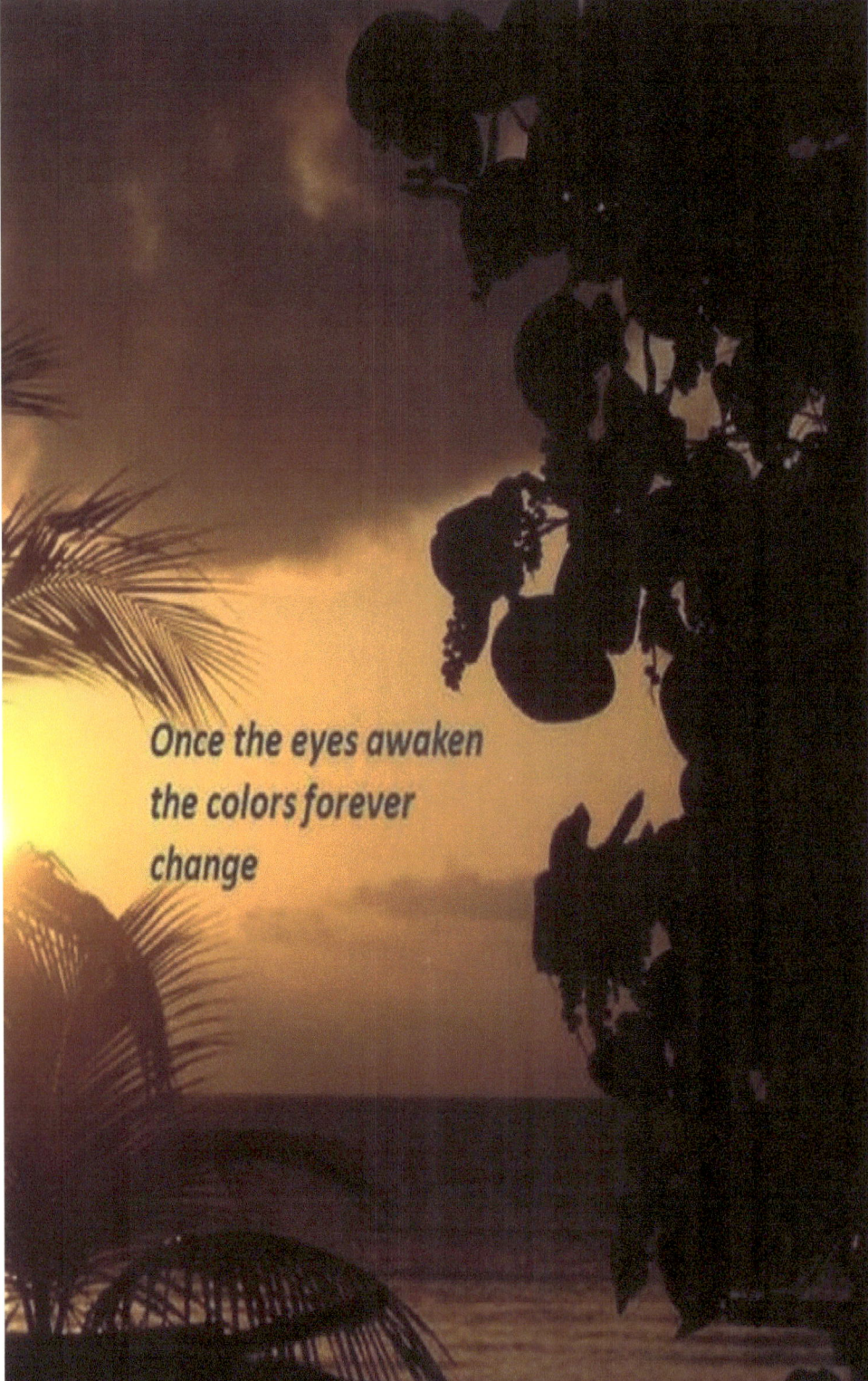

To My Family And Friends

This, the sum of my life story and passion for life, is to be dedicated to my loved ones.

First and foremost, I live for my children and my grandchildren. I'd like to thank my daughter Autumn and her older sister Amy for always believing in me and helping me to reach my dreams. These girls are amazing despite being so different, one working in the trades and the other aiming for a PhD in the Social Sciences. These kids have positive energy to bring to the world!

I'd also like to dedicate this text to my grandson Sammy, who turned two years old recently. The light he has brought to my family's eyes and hearts has been absolutely dazzling truly has my father's spirit in him.

Speaking of my father, I also dedicate this book to my late parents, Samuel and Ida. One I lost early, the other I lost way too recently. Both brought joy to the people around them, with my father having a most adventurous spirit and a character tested by deployment to Asia twice during the Cold War. He lived and died on his own terms and was proud of it. My mother was largely a product of years of pioneering and the Church of Jesus Christ of Latter Day Saints, but tragically left us when I was but a little girl due to childhood trauma.

I'd also like to dedicate this work to my older brothers Samuel and Steve.

Of course this dedication would be nothing without mentioning my husband Ronnie. Thank you for being you, and for letting me be myself.

A special part of me carries the spirit of my Grandma Lola. Thank you so much, you took over for my mother and taught me how the world works. I'm grateful you got to meet your great-grandchildren.

I'd like to thank the Holden Beach community for providing me a peaceful, relaxed place to heal.

Last but not least, I would like to thank the Lord Jesus Christ.

"And he said unto me, It is done. I am Alpha and Omega, the beginning and the end.
I will give unto him that is thirsty of the fountain of the water of life freely."
- Book of Revelations 21:6

Mystery in Nature

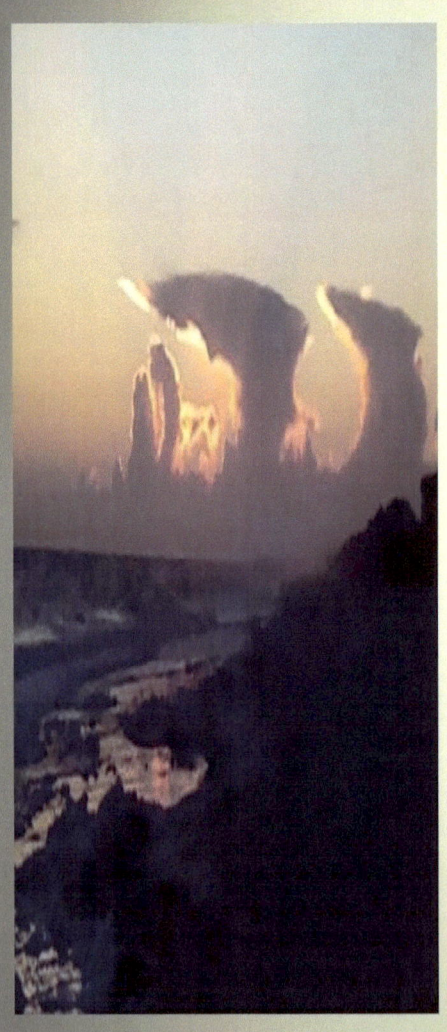

At times, the skies looked as if Dragons were playing on earths crest..

Needles from pine straw dancing with our Moon

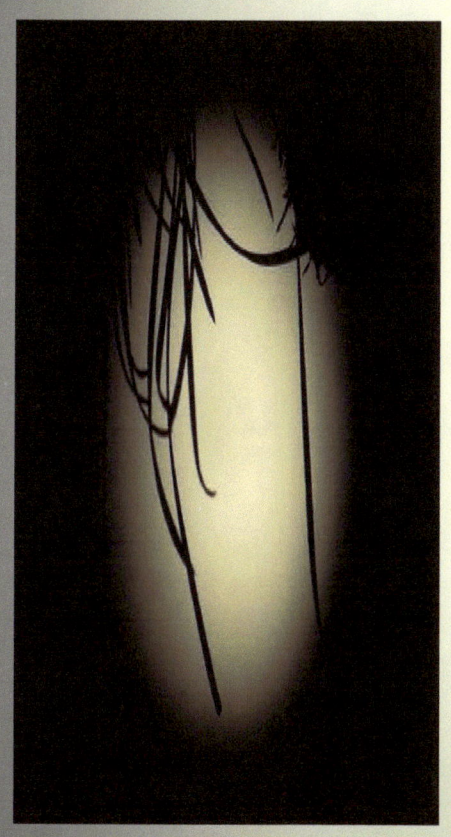

If we stop to look, there is beauty all around.

Possibilities are Limitless

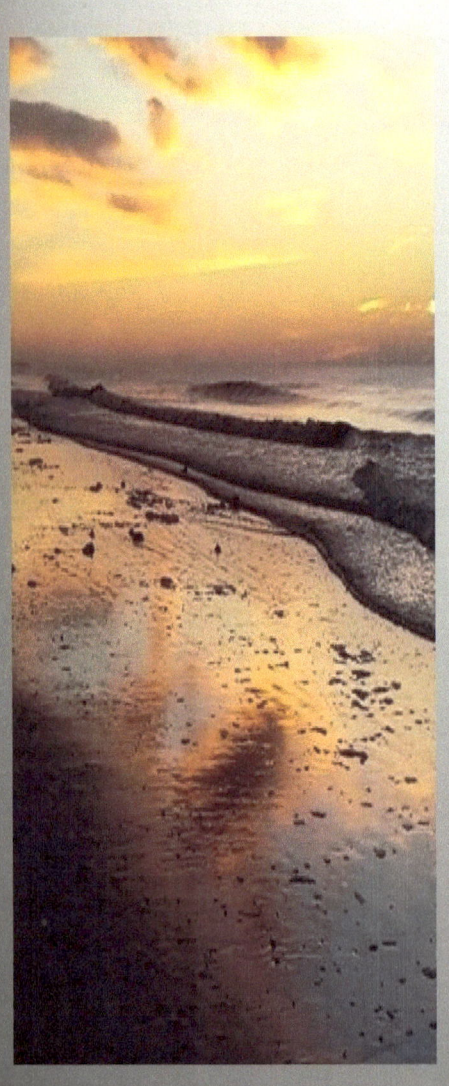

- *It's the digging deep, it's the letting go of what society has told us to do and allowing our inner spirit to just spill out.*

Bubbles

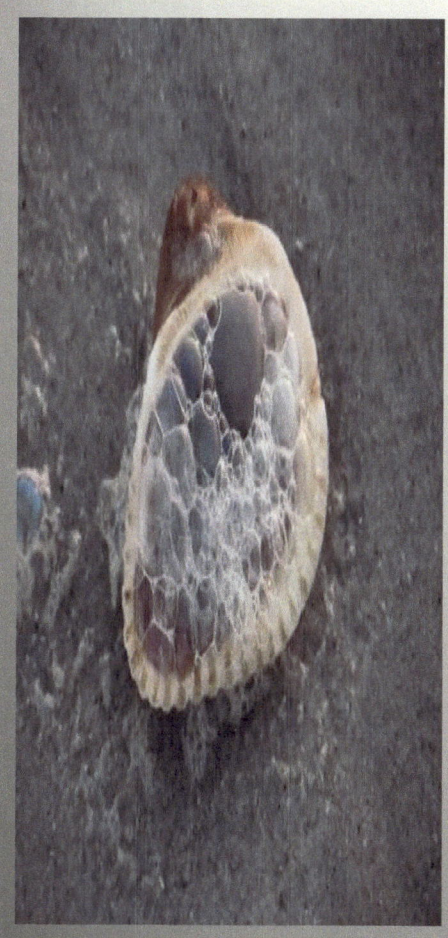

The universe bursts into existence from life, not the other way around as we have been taught. For each life there is a universe, its own universe. We generate spheres of reality, individual bubbles of existence. Our planet is comprised of billions of spheres of reality, generated by each individual human and perhaps even by each animal.

Robert Lanza

In the Moments

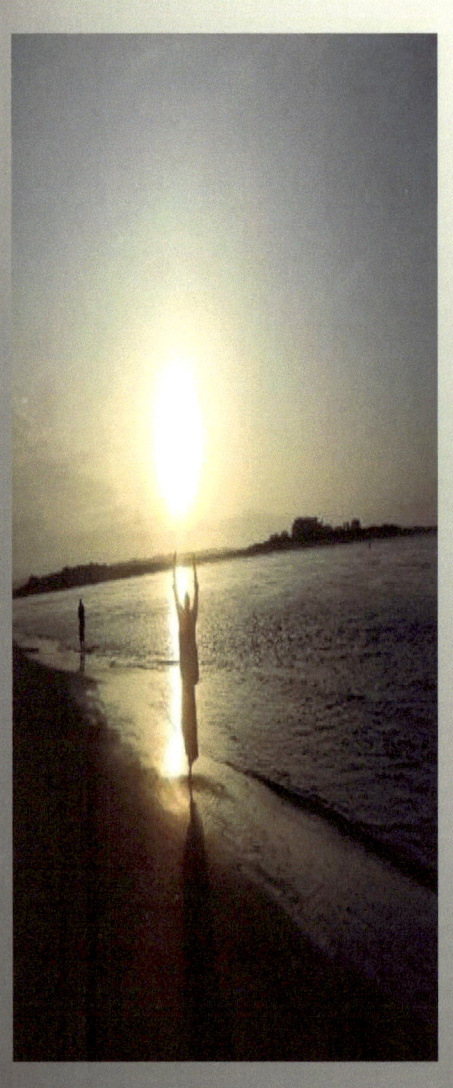

- *This transition will take me to places I've only dreamed of in my wee world.*

Views on Technology

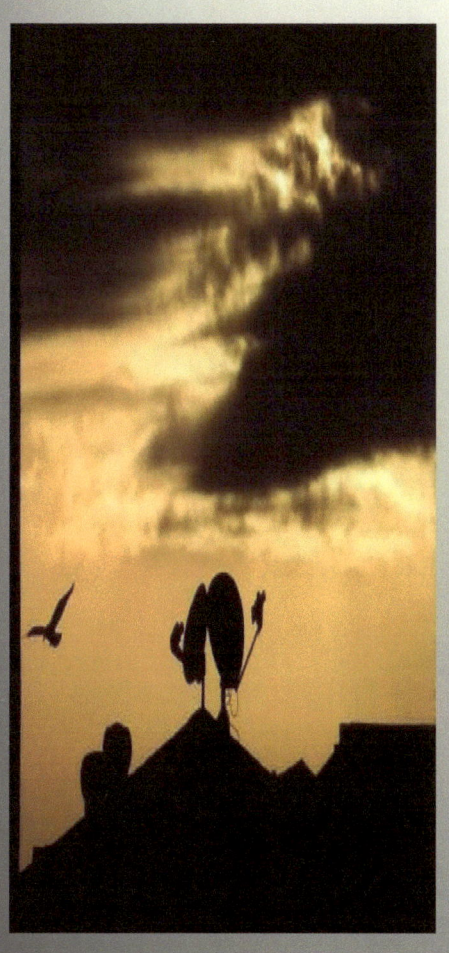

"We are an impossibility in an impossible universe."

— Ray Bradbury

Patterns in Nature

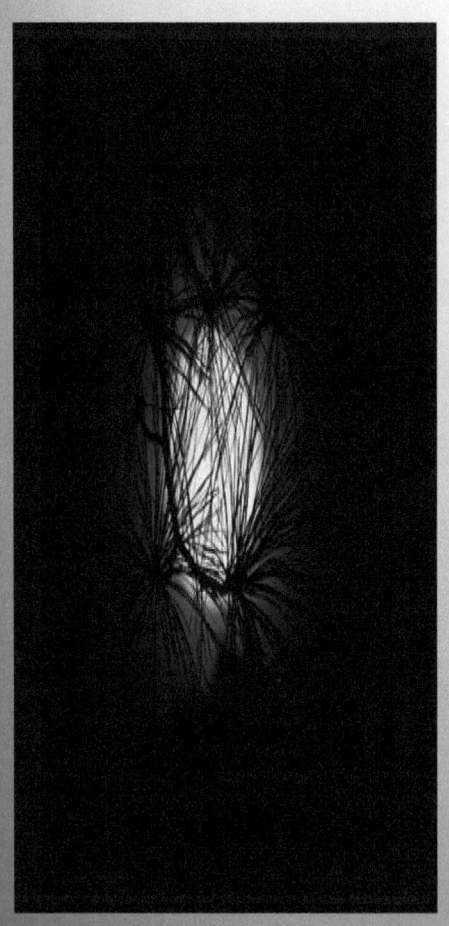

The patterns in life are all connected, as they are in nature. Seeing and hearing these energies tis what keeps one in tune....

Always look deep into the abyss

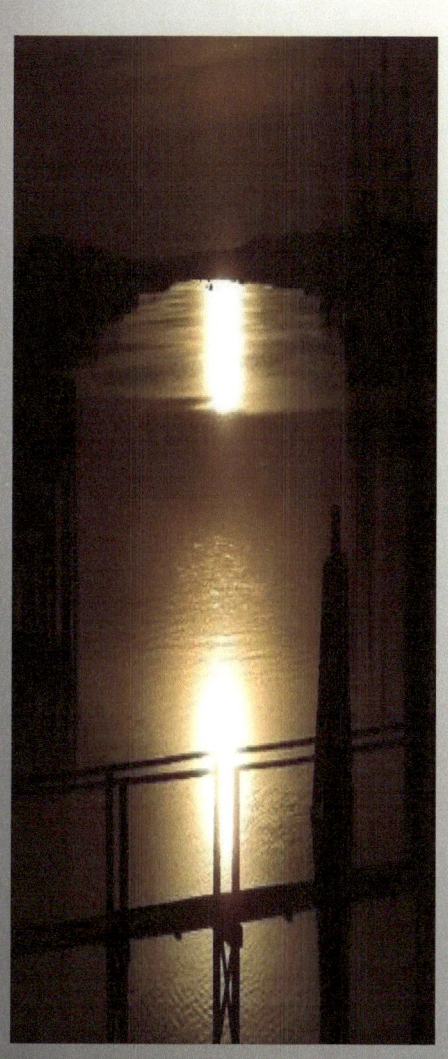

- *When channeling in life, taking a break from reality. Remember to look beyond what is right in front of our eyes, only then will the real message appear.*

Sacred Geometry

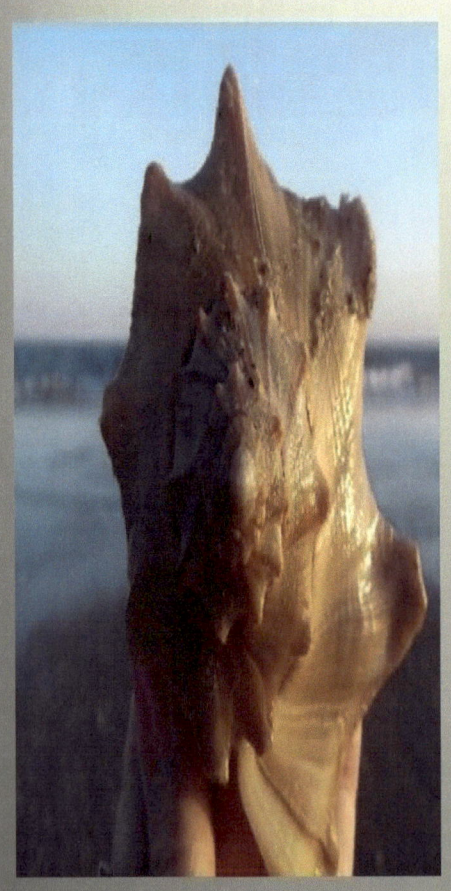

We are so connected with nature, just look at this conch shell and picture the Cochlea of an inner ear.

Red Sky Delight

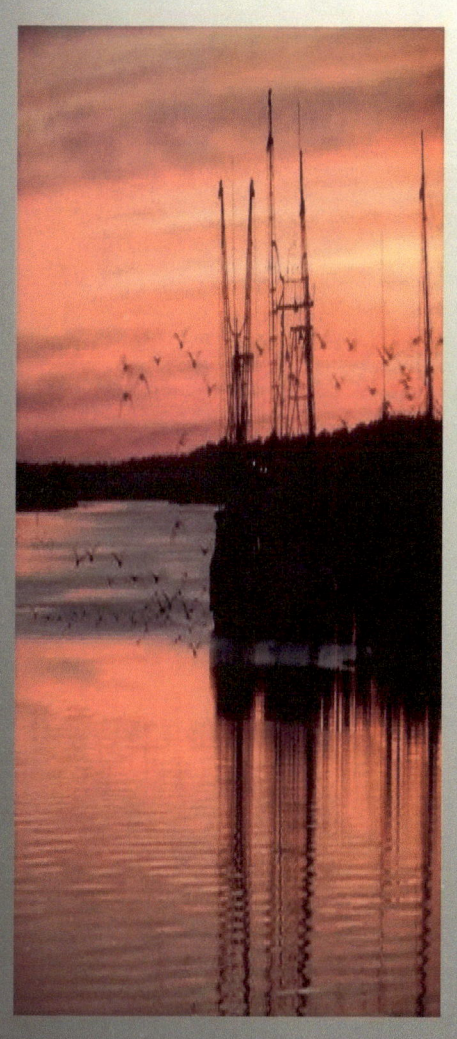

Free therapy in nature, one must disconnect in order to see this type of beauty.

Peering through a Pier

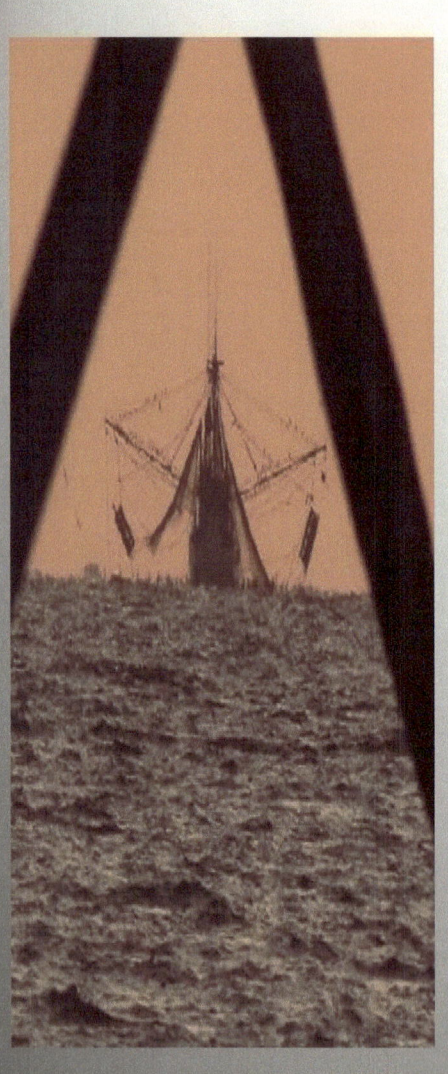

- *Learning and growing is kind of like fishing or shrimping. We search for a catch, load it up then start all over again!*

Ghosted Shrimp Yard

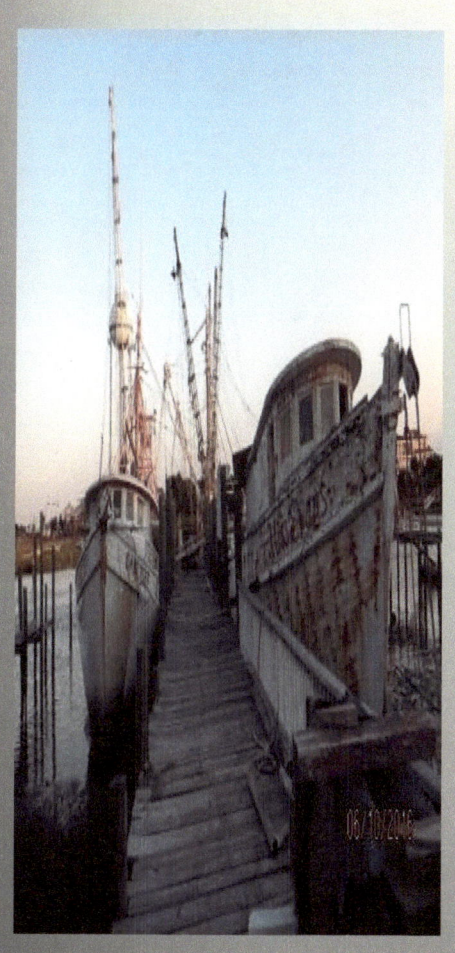

"She says she glories in being abandoned"

– J.M. Barrie

Learn to fly

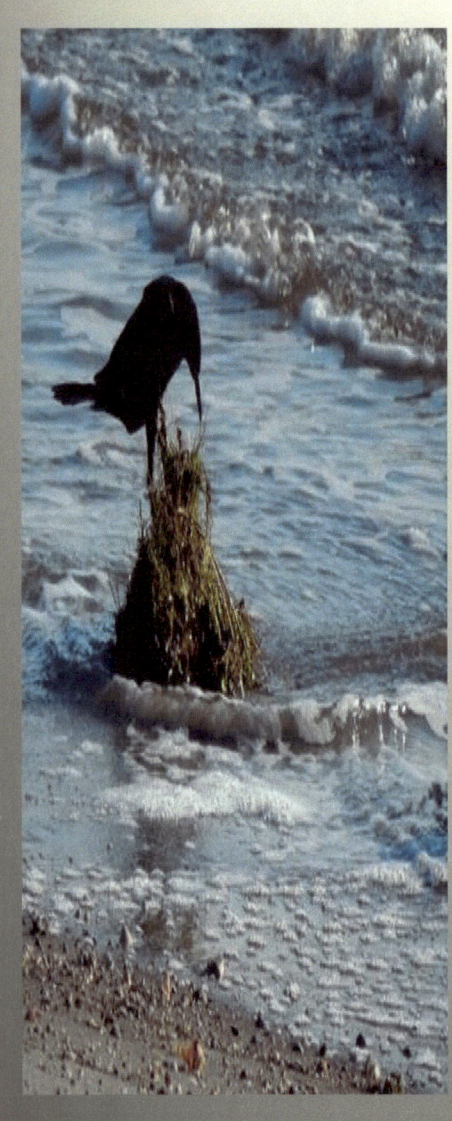

- *The cancer gave me the push needed to pull away from what was laid on me at birth. No one writes our scripts in life, that journey is ours to explore.*

Ms. Hairy

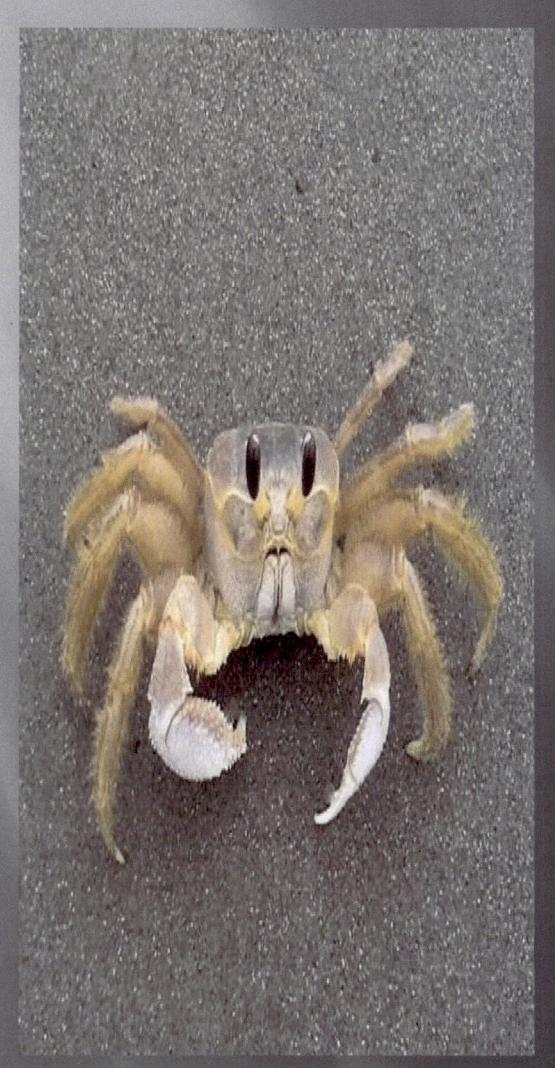

- Staying in a small studio ocean front. Early one morning while awaiting the sunrise, this little creature and I danced freely on the beach.

Embrace the wrong turns

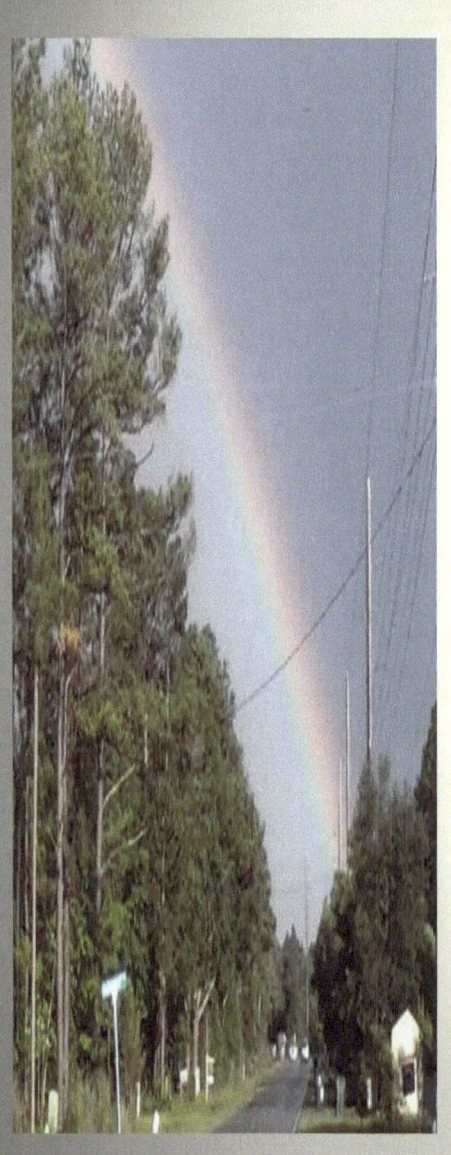

- *Another lesson from Cancer, the chemotherapy zapped my directional skills. This was a wrong turn which lead a friend and I right into a beautiful double rainbow.*

A key in Nesting

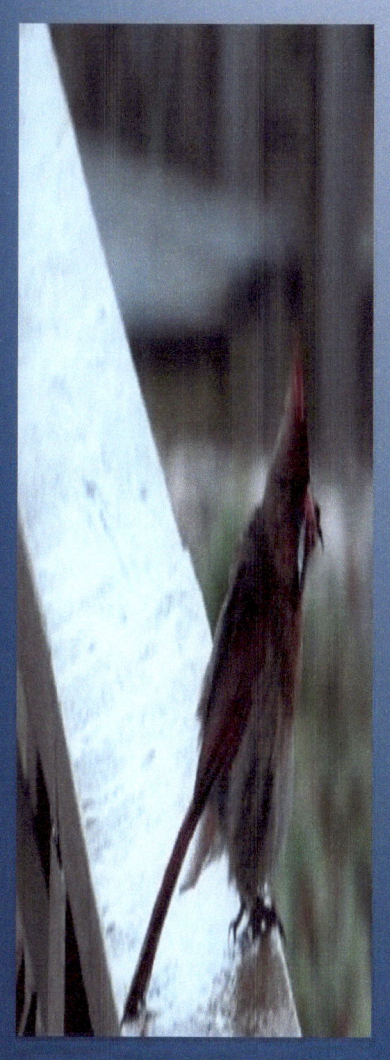

- *No matter where your journey may lay the head, nesting is so important. Grab the surroundings close in, embrace the beauty that is around us.*

Structural Clarity

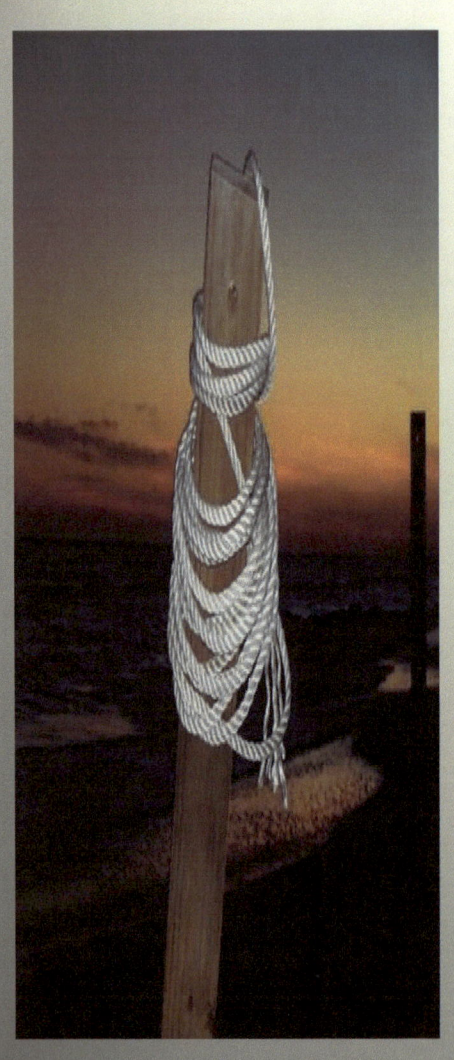

- *WE are born to stand out! Man has created this system using us to turn a wheel. Grab your rope, believe in yourself.*

Cotton Candy on the Rise

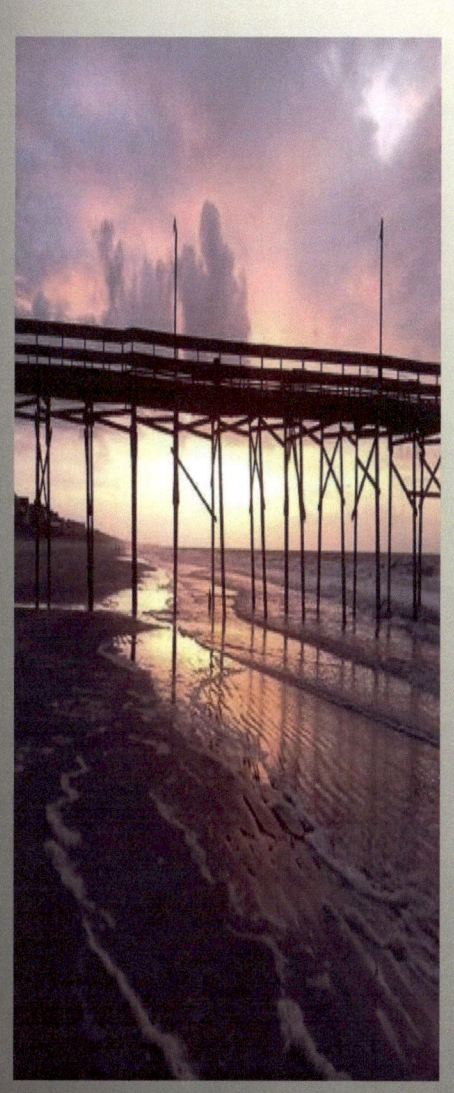

- *The only constant in life is change. To embrace that frees one up, opens the eyes to see the ever changing colors and beauty that surrounds us all.....*

Always Stay on Point

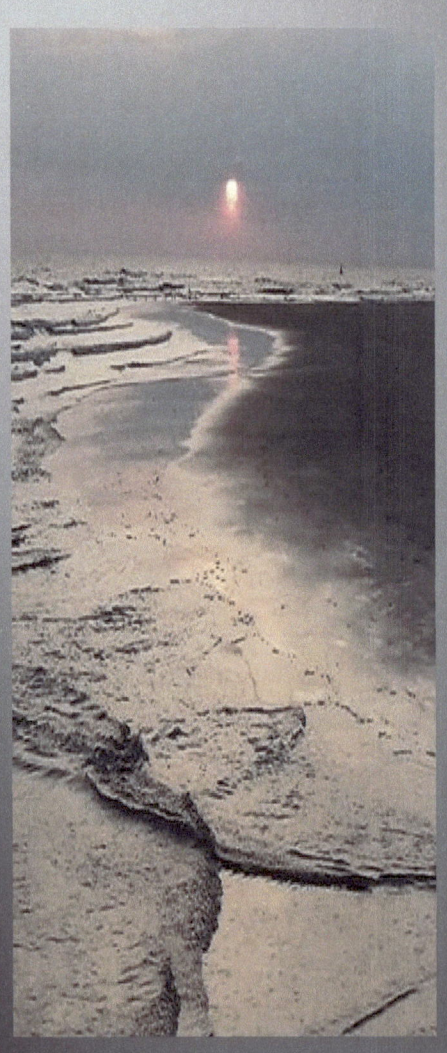

Staying centered, staying on point takes courage at times and sometimes courage is all we have.

Dew Right

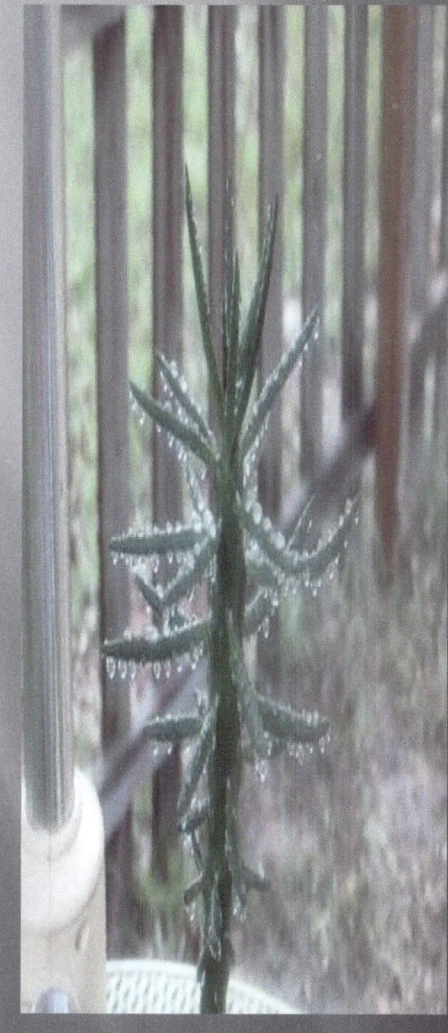

Sometimes we just need to be still as the dew settles.

Embrace the Eclipse's in Life

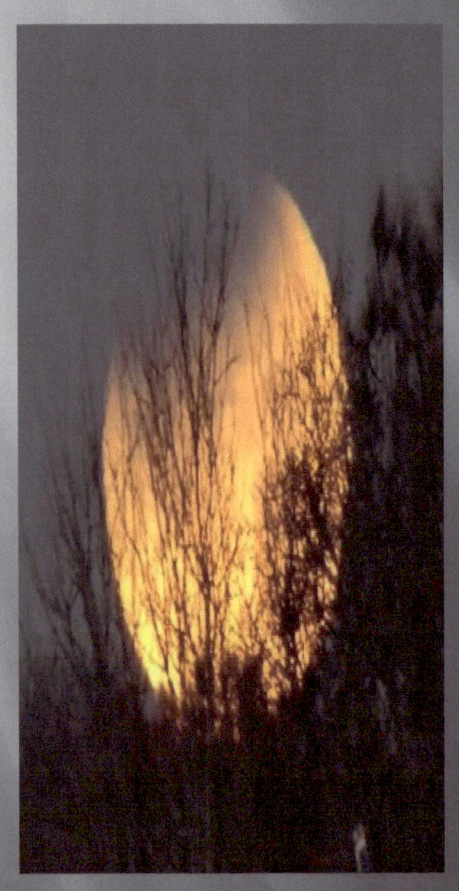

When dark clouds show up and they will, take the time to nurture the darker side of ourselves. Most times these came from childhood trauma and can be healed.

Stay Rooted

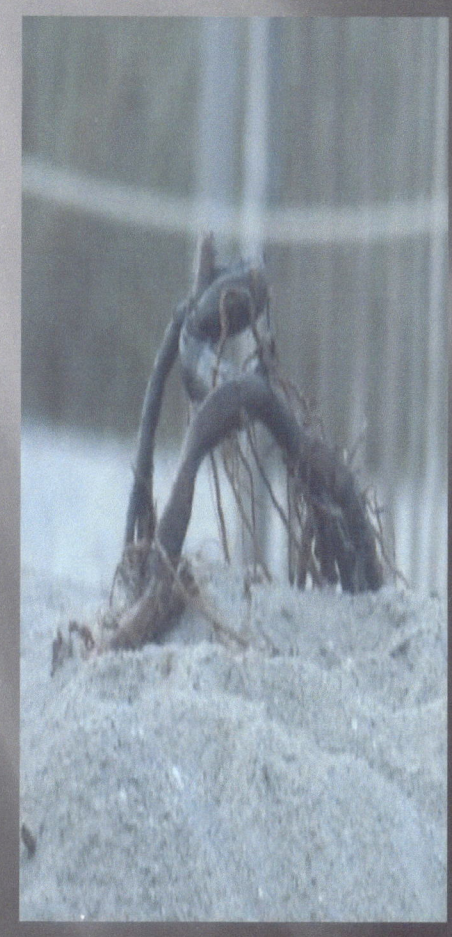

To stay rooted, to keep a strong foundation we must be grounded with nature.

A Different Perspective

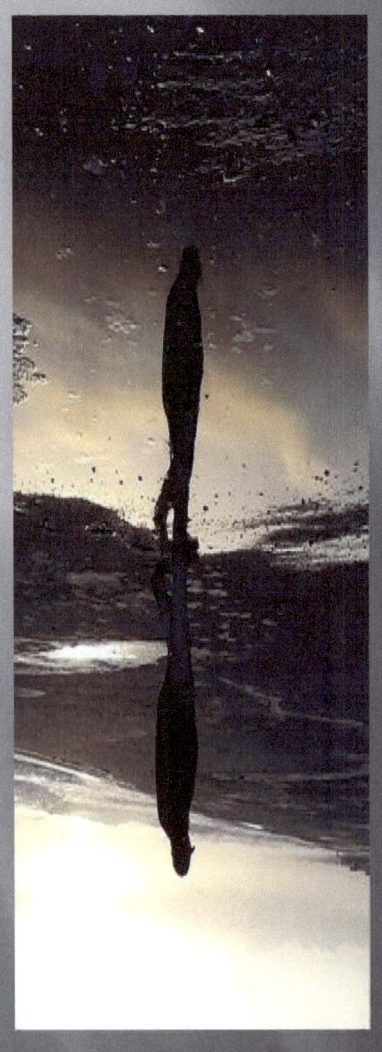

Most times we just need to step back and get a different perspective of each situation.

Once We Hear

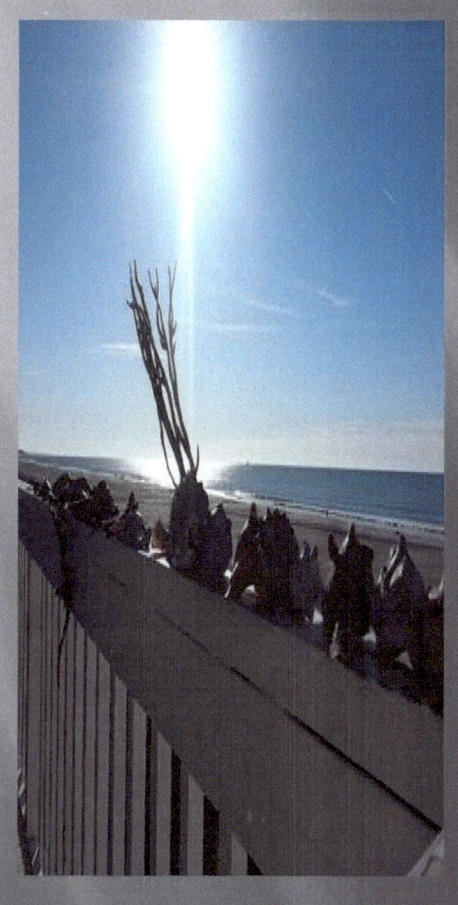

Once we open our eyes and hear the word then it may be time to silence our brains a bit and absorb the newly founded freedom.

Be Supported

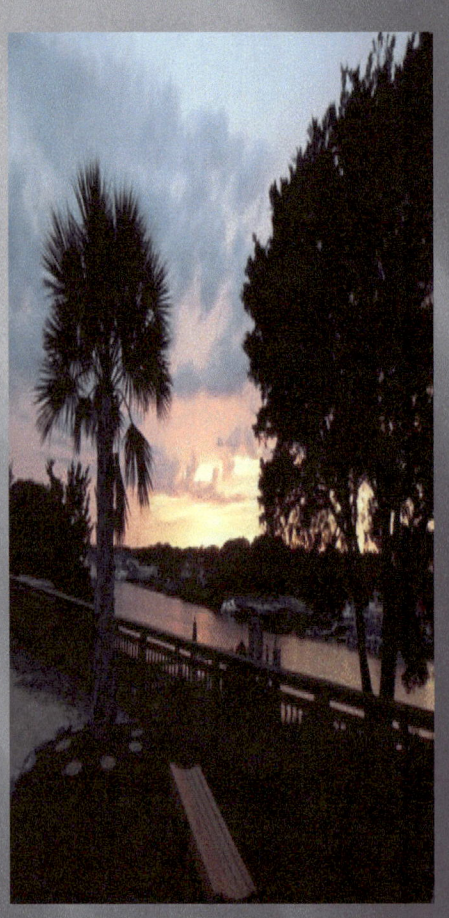

If you feel yourself floundering in life, try leaning back and floating. Be supported by nature, lean back and gaze into the sky and allow time for your spirit to be refreshed.

Love Others

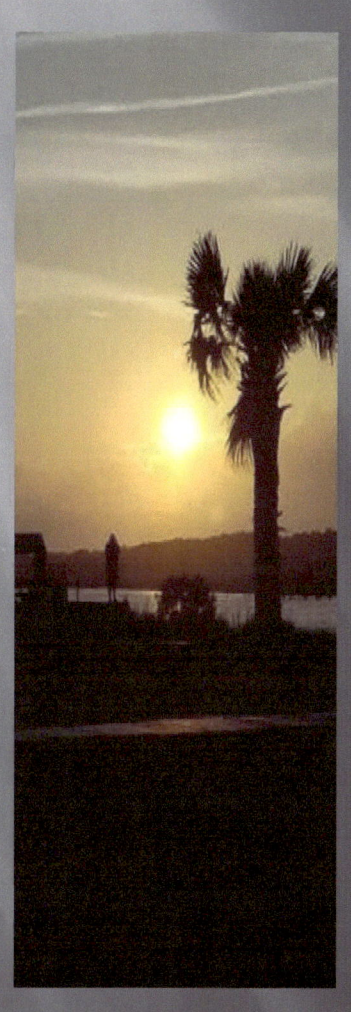

How are others whom don't love themselves suppose to understand love unless we give it? If we are speaking of our brothers or sisters in haste please stop and let us train our tongues to only speak the best and healing side of all.

Freedom from the Storms

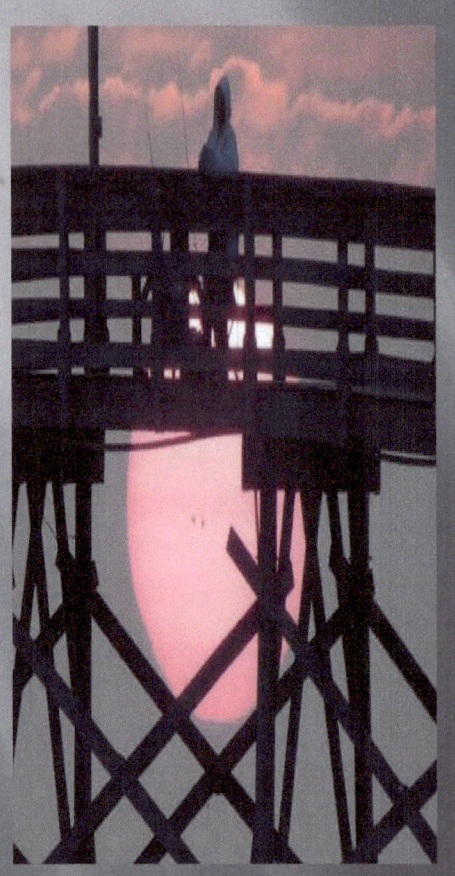

The storms which used to cover her were erased magically with each step into the abyss. It was there she finally made that "Be Still" connection with God.

www.ingramcontent.com/pod-product-compliance
Lightning Source LLC
Chambersburg PA
CBHW041949240526
45473CB00036B/2793